SMART
MONEY

8 STRATEGIES FOR FINANCIAL
SECURITY, SUCCESS AND
SIGNIFICANCE

CURTIS R. ESTES

I must credit divine inspiration for the creation of this book. It came to mind, fully formed, upon waking on April 8, 2017, in the middle of the Caribbean on an amazing spring break cruise with my family.

As I began writing, I smiled at the crazy coincidence that my daughter is eleven, and I knew that the timing was not a coincidence.

I count my blessings every day that my daughter didn't have to go through the horrific challenges that I did at the age of eleven.

This book, then, is dedicated to the world's eleven-year-old children. May we all protect them each and every day.

Smart Money: 8 Strategies for Financial Security, Success, and Significance

Contents

Introduction

Since my childhood, I have been drawn to and captivated by people who "had it together" from a financial perspective. My Uncle John had a chain of pharmacies and flew his own airplane. My Aunt Anna was the first female top executive at a public company in Kansas City. My Los Angeles mentor, Dana Anderson, took Macerich public on the New York Stock Exchange—and it is now an $8 billion company and the third largest owner and operator of shopping centers in the United States.

Why do some people do so well with their money while others destroy themselves?

That was the question I needed to answer since the time I was eleven years old.

Section 1
8 Questions for Financial Security

When I was eleven years old, my house burned to the ground on Christmas Day.

We had no fire insurance, and we were left with almost nothing. We moved into a trailer house, and just about everything we had was donated by friends from our church. My "back to school" clothes came from the Salvation Army.

For a lower-middle-class family of four, the financial loss was huge. My mom was too proud to sign us up for the free lunch at school, so she took three jobs, including one as a housekeeper. As soon as we could work, my sister and I got jobs flipping burgers alongside my mom at McDonalds.

My parents' relationship had been strained for years, and after the fire, it never recovered. They separated three years later and ultimately divorced.

In some ways, these experiences were positive in that I learned a lot about what matters most, what I wanted to do differently, and how I would never put my kids through the same financial devastation that tore apart my childhood.

Yet, I also have the perspective of what life could have been like if only we had been protected. Having served thousands of clients as a financial planning professional over the last 26 years, I am the guy who shows up with a big check in hand. When I speak with grieving spouses, the sentiment is often the same.

The two thoughts I hear most often are:

- "I never thought this would happen to me," and
- "I am overwhelmed by the future, but at least I don't have to worry about money."

While my parents didn't die during the fire, so much joy died on that Christmas Day. As much as I learned from the experience, I wish I could rewind time and introduce my parents to someone like me when I was ten years old—or, even better, right when I was born. If I could prevent that fire, I would trade all of the ensuing lessons to protect my mom, my sister, my dad, and myself from the financial and personal strain that arose.

When my parents bought the home that later burned to the ground, they had discussed fire insurance with several professionals, but they always postponed action, thinking they would be better able to afford it down the road. Instead, they lost everything, and they never recovered.

The purpose of this book, then, is to jolt you into awareness so that you do the planning that you want to do—now. I have had more than 20,000 financial planning meetings, and I have counseled many people with the same hopes, dreams, and challenges as you. I have seen too many people make the same decision my parents made, and with similar disastrous results.

I have heard through the grapevine that the "too-busy-to-get-to-it" dad was diagnosed with early onset multiple sclerosis. I have heard that the "don't-need-it" stay-at-home mom just learned she has terminal cancer. I have heard about the parents who died in sudden car accidents and whose young children were left with few resources.

I want to help you do everything that is within your control to protect your family, no matter the outside circumstances. You have a choice to make for you and your family. You can live your life by default, allowing outside circumstances to dictate your future, or you can live your life by design, taking control of your future to the best of your ability.

I'm going to give you eight questions you can ask to lead you closer to financial security. Then, I'm going to give you a few strategies on how to have the mindset to achieve and also sustain your goals. Finally, I'll share a few ways to not only have a much bigger future for you and your family, but also for the next generation and for your legacy.

The strategies I share can be both the rocket fuel and the security net to enjoy the fruit of your labor and provide an enduring example of financial wisdom as a priceless legacy to your children.

In other words, these strategies teach you how to be smart with your money, moving to success and significance.

●●●●●●

Listening to my parents fighting about money was brutal, particularly because my dad took progressively less responsibility after the crushing financial and emotional impact of the fire. He became more and more distant from us, often leaving us over the Christmas season without much explanation—and without enough wood to keep the fireplace burning so that our house could warm during the cold winter nights.

Yet, as I wrote earlier, I am grateful in a sense for the experiences I had while growing up. There is no doubt that I landed in the financial security business as a direct reaction to growing up with no financial security.

There is also no doubt that, because of this experience, I witnessed a person's ability to rise above any circumstance and to choose heroism instead of victimhood. Through it all, my mom never complained. She flipped burgers with her teenage kids and their friends, and she did it with a smile. She cleaned houses, grateful for the job. And as soon as we left for college, she earned her nursing degree. To this day, at the age of 74, she works as a nurse in a drug rehab facility.

Each day, my mom demonstrates how hard work and a positive attitude translate into a great life. She has been the role model for me, and she is the role model for all of her patients, many of whom have hit bottom themselves.

I want you to be the victor and enjoy financial security without having to hit bottom. My goal is to pass along the wisdom I have gained from my 20,000 meetings, learning from the clients who made the important choices to sacrifice a little bit now to insure their family's financial security for decades to come.

In other words, I am the advocate for your future self.

And to be certain, your future self will likely have a slightly different perspective than today's self. Generally, people spend their twenties and thirties blissfully unaware of anything that could go wrong. This attitude starts to change during their forties and fifties, and by the time they are sixty or seventy, they see how important proper planning is. They either struggle with making the hard choices between getting the health care they need or maintaining quality of life (if they failed to plan), or they count their blessings that they planned for the future during prior decades.

This book reflects on the many open conversations I have had with clients of all stages of life—those who have wondered if the stock market would ever bounce back after "the Great Recession," those who fought through health issues, those who lost family members suddenly and unexpectedly, and those who prayed that their teenagers would make good decisions for themselves. The strategies are based on these conversations, and the lessons I have learned from those who choose the path of victory for their future self.

Through a series of questions, we will start by covering eight foundational strategies that undergird financial security and set you up to enjoy success, and move you beyond success and toward significance.

Question 1: "What am I most excited about?"

I have hosted more than 100 private dinners in a secret room in a Beverly Hills restaurant. The main takeaway that I want for the guests who attend the dinner is this: Identify what they are most excited about.

Toward that objective, I always start the dinners with this question: "What are you most excited about?"

These dinners are always extraordinary because people are eager to share what they are most excited about. We spend so much time putting out fires and managing day-to-day minutia that we have little time or energy left for talking about what excites us. When I ask this question, then, I see a shift in people's minds. They become reflective. They sit with their thoughts, dig deep, and remember their truest desires. Even the most introverted guests share something exciting about themselves and their bigger future.

The dinners are special because we are given a window into the best of who the other guests are, and, more importantly, who they are becoming.

Who are you becoming?

Answering this first question might not be an obvious step toward securing your financial future, but it is the most important one. The key to starting this adventure is to get really clear about what you are most excited about.

If you are having a hard time answering this question, re-phrase it like this: "How would I describe my most amazing future?"

> **A dear friend always says that with a big enough *why*, then *how* doesn't matter.**

A dear friend always says that with a big enough *why*, then *how* doesn't matter. I must agree. I would never cross a plank spanning the top of twin 100-story skyscrapers on my own accord, but if my unstoppable toddler scampered across the same narrow plank while chasing a butterfly, I would run right behind her, without question, desperate to rescue her from a deadly fall.

As this example shows, with a big enough *why*, then *how* truly doesn't matter.

Answering this chapter's question helps you identify your bigger *why*. Why would you cross the plank spanning the sky scrapers? You likely would not do it to make an extra buck, but you certainly would to save a loved one.

Here is my answer to the question ...

My bigger *why* is always this: I want to make sure I have done a great job of providing for my family. What am I most excited about? I love thinking about the future that my children and my wife have, and, God willing, the amazing adventure we will have together. Having experienced the worst of financial negligence, I never want my family to endure the hardships that I did. I want the opposite for them, and I am driven by the promise of watching joy spread across their faces as they experience the best of life.

In addition to making sure my family does not end up in a trailer home, I want to teach them to value their experiences. We just spent a weekend building a home for a needy family in Tijuana through Homes for Hope. Every week, Homes for Hope takes businesses, churches, and groups of friends across the border to build homes for just $8,000 each.

Homes for Hope has built over 5,000 homes so far, one of which was built by my family. It was an incredible experience to share with my kids, one of whom did not want to go, but who had an incredible transformation of heart and spirit. By day two, he was on the roof nailing down the shingles.

This kind of lesson is impossible to teach with a school book. (Check out the link on our website to learn more if you're interested: ywamsandiegobaja.org/homesofhope/.)

I was once told that our children are the most powerful message we get to send to future generations. I want to raise Jordan, Vyvien and Christian to be grateful, ingenious, value creators in their lives and as an example to our grandkids.

If you could wave the proverbial magic wand, what would your most exciting future look like? Simply by writing it down with as much vivid, descriptive detail as you can, you will be one step closer toward making your dream a reality.

Share what you are most excited about. If you could design your ideal future, what would it look like?

What am I most excited about?

_____

_____

_____

_____

_____

_____

_____

_____

_____

_____

_____

_____

_____

_____

_____

_____

_____

As a thank you for your interest in *Smart Money*, I'd like to share the first seven chapters of each of my prior two books:

- *Your Life by Design: A Step-by-Step Guide to Creating Your Bigger Future.* This book walks you through the entire process of getting clear about your bigger future. You will create an action plan for fast results and arrive at your life by design sooner than anyone expects. Please go to www.yourlifebydesignbook.com.

- *Family First: How to Be a Hero at Home.* Far from being a story about how good I am, *Family First* is more of a confession about how I realized I was not being the husband and father that I wanted to be. I figured that writing a book about my vision and efforts to be a much better dad was the best form of accountability I could have. Check it out at www.familyfirstbook.com.

Question 2: "What matters most?"

As you can read in *Family First*, I have been a disaster as a husband and a father as often as I have been a good example. Though I am still working every day to be a better spouse and dad, one thing is certain: I am not perfect, but I love my family with all of my heart.

And I am sure you love your family just as much as much as I love mine.

So the second question—"What matters most?"—is rhetorical. I already know what matters most: Your family.

Because they matter most, make sure they are properly insured. I know firsthand how much a family can lose—financially, emotionally, and relationally—without proper financial planning.

As a foundational priority, make sure that you have the right amount of life insurance. My clients consistently tell me that they want their life insurance to do three things for them:

1. They want their life insurance to cover their mortgage and debts.
2. They want education fully funded for their kids.
3. They want to replace a portion of each breadwinner's income so that the family can enjoy the same standard of living in the event of one parent's death.

Living in Los Angeles is not cheap, so Kristi and I want $1 million to cover the mortgage. We want $500,000 (times three) to cover the private school educations for our children's high school and college. We also want an additional $1 million of insurance for every $2,500 I earn monthly. This means we would want $10 million if my monthly salary were $25,000.

(A standard that may be used: In a low-interest-rate environment, assuming 3 percent on safely invested dollars, it takes an additional $1 million of insurance proceeds to replace $30,000 per year, or $2,500 of income per month.)

Fortunately, $12.5 million of term insurance is relatively inexpensive, as I will explain later. For now, let's talk about how to skimp on life insurance.

If you were to die, perhaps your spouse would move or re-marry, which means you can lower the amount of life insurance that is necessary, right?

That may very well be true, but I, for one, do not want my wife to remarry just so that she can provide for the kids. I also do not want her to move, or pull the kids out of school, particularly if they are grieving. I want my children and my wife to be comforted by the community, friends, church, and neighbors we love so much

If I die, I want my family to enjoy the same standard of living as they do with me around. I want them to make great memories from enjoying fun vacations. I want them to continue with their summer camps and extra-curricular activities. I want to leave a legacy of providing the best for my family and giving them every opportunity to leave an inspiring legacy for generations to come.

For those reasons, I have chosen not to skimp on my own life insurance.

Of course, if your spouse does not bring home an income, you might not need to cover your spouse, right? If you do not have children, or if you have grown children, this might be true, but consider why life insurance is important if you have young children.

Having a meaningful amount of life insurance on Kristi means that if anything happens to her, I can dramatical-ly reduce my obligations at work so I that I can step in as substitute for some of the time she spends with our chil-dren. I would want to take them to school, pick them up, and attend the non-stop sporting events and parent teacher conferences.

I would be unable to do that if I did not have life insurance on Kristi. In essence, her life insurance would cover the lost income that would occur when I cut back on work to give my children the love and support they would need.

There are two general types of life insurance: term and permanent. Term insurance is quite inexpensive (assuming you have good health). You pay a fixed premium for a fixed rate of time. If you die during this time, your family receives the payout. If you are still living at the end of the term, the policy is terminated without any payout.

In another section, we will talk about permanent life insurance, the second kind, but for now, let's make sure you cover what matters most, with the appropriate amount of protection.

To determine how much life insurance you need, visit calculator.northwesternmutual.com/response/lf-northwesternmutual/calc/lifeins01, or use the worksheet on the next page.

This is just an estimation: It's always best to consult with a financial planning professional to determine the exact numbers appropriate for your situation.

For more information on the use of life insurance as a foundational piece of your financial security plan, please visit: northwesternmutual.com/products-and-services/life-insurance.

How Much Life Insurance Do I Need?

Add the expenses listed in this first table to get the capital needed.

Existing mortgage or the rent/mortgage on the home you would want to provide for your family:	
Debt:	+
Remaining pre-school through 12 education for children:	+
Children's college:	+
$1M for each $2,500/month of each breadwinner's income to be replaced (typically 60 to 80 percent)[1]:	+
Total capital needed.	=

Once you have the total capital needed, subtract your available assets.

Total capital needed:	−
Current life insurance protection:	−
Liquid assets:	−
The after-tax value of qualified retirement assets:	−
The amount of life insurance you need.	=

---

1   http://money.cnn.com/2015/07/22/retirement/retirement-income/index.html

Question 3: "Do I have a documented estate plan to pass on my money and my values?"

Let's start with the money.

Not having an estate plan for your assets is a problem for several reasons. First, if you have not elected guardians for your children and you die, the courts will decide who raises your children. All your friends, family members, and non-friends alike can step forward and nominate themselves, and a judge—who likely has different values and priorities than you have—will decide who will raise your children.

And, even if your wishes for the transfer of your money are outlined in a will, your money will not transfer until your estate has been through probate—unless you have a trust.

Therefore, you need two sets of documents:

1. A will specifying your wishes with respect to your children and your assets, as well as
2. A trust, which manages the money and, in many cases, keeps your estate out of probate.

Many parents intuitively know that they should have some basic estate planning like this done, but most haven't gotten around to it yet. Don't let this be you. Email me at curtis.estes@nm.com, and I would be glad to leverage our national network to connect you with several competent attorneys in your area.

In addition to the basics, there are extraordinary planning opportunities available as your success grows. The reality is that there are many ways to reduce estate taxes with advanced strategies by using a quality estate planning attorney. My friend likes to say that he's happy to pay his fair share to the IRS but he doesn't need to tip.[2]

If Kristi and I did no planning, after adding our life insurance to our other assets, we would be subject to a hefty "tip to the IRS" in estate taxes. As such, I have worked with an attorney to create a "zero estate tax plan." Here are the details:

We want to incentivize our kids, but we do not want to ruin them either. Within the current gift exclusion amounts we have identified the amount we want to give the kids to make sure that they have adequate resources to put a down payment on a home, start a business, and launch them into a productive adulthood. This amount is high enough to be an incentive but low enough to keep our children working and productive.

We've also set aside money to help with grandkids' education and the charities that mean so much to us.

Between the current exemption and our life insurance, all these legacy goals are fully funded.

---

2   Please email me if your net worth is more than $10 million, and through our national network, I'll be glad to introduce you to several tax attorneys who will make sure your hard-earned dollars go exactly where you want.

The remaining estate value will be given to a donor-advised fund that is tax exempt. As a family, we make charitable gifts from the fund. After we die, the children will continue to manage this together as part of their example of philanthropy for their children.

With this plan, we anticipate that there will be no estate taxes, no matter how much wealth we are able to accumulate.

Don't Forget the Values Side of the Plan
It's essential to realize that your estate plan does not end with a written will and trust documents. These documents prepare the money to be transferred, but they do not prepare your heirs for the money, which is arguably more important.

Therefore, your written estate plan should also include a "values" plan to prepare your heirs for money. We go into more detail in section three, but this is a good primer.

You may have heard of the adage "shirtsleeves to shirtsleeves in three generations." Over 90 percent of traditional completed estate plans fail (Cochell, Perry and Zeeb, Rod. *Beating the Midas Curse*. GenUs, 2013.), not for lack of the documents, but because the well-intentioned parents have not intentionally and diligently passed onto their heirs their stories, values, and life lessons, in addition to their money.

When money is the primary focus of estate planning, inheritors often equate their self-worth with their net worth. There's been a lot of talk in recent years about the rich kid disease of "affluenza." When children inherit money without

appreciating the efforts of earning it, they can have a dys-
functional relationship with the money resulting in such outcomes as the inability to delay gratification, low self-esteem,
lack of personal identity, and a false sense of entitlement.

In other words, children born on the third base mistake that
for hitting a triple.

Affluenza's surest cure is active philanthropy. Just two weeks
ago, we saw this with the dramatic change of heart in our
son, who did not want to build homes in Tijuana, until he
was sitting atop a roof with nails in hand. From this, and
many other experiences, we have developed a passion for
actively giving away as much as we can to meet the incredible immediate needs around us and see the impact during
our life time.

The pastor Rick Warren inspired us by his example. Pastor
Warren decided to increase his annual giving by 1 percent
each year. Currently, we are giving away double digits of our
income. One day, we hope to give away 90 percent of our
income and live off 10 percent.

I share this story because I believe that you will be better off
if you have an actionable plan to prepare your family members for their financial inheritance. As Christians, Kristi and
I believe that everything we have is a gift, and that we are
blessed to be a blessing to others. Therefore, we model this
for our children.

As part of my planning and advisory services, I help clients discover, articulate, and share how they will prepare their family for the wealth they will inherit. You may have done a great job of financial and estate planning, but have you also prepared your children for the inheritance they will receive as a result of that planning?

Financial estate planning checklist:

☐ **Create an Inventory of What You Own and What You Owe.** There are many good reasons to compile a comprehensive list of your assets and debts, including account numbers and contact information, as well as names and contact information for your important advisers. The Northwestern Mutual Guide for the Future (available at www.northwesternmutual.com/learning-center/brochures) is a tool for summarizing that information and saving it electronically. Keep the summary in a secure, central location—along with original copies of important documents—and provide a copy of the summary for the executor of your will.

☐ **Develop a Contingency Plan.** An estate plan allows you to control what would happen to your property and assets if you or your spouse passed away today. It also puts a documented plan in place so that if you became incapacitated, your family could carry on your affairs without having to go through court. This includes a strategy for providing income if you were to become disabled and covering potential expenses for care, given that it may be needed at some point.

☐ **Provide for Children and Dependents.** A primary goal for many estate plans is to protect and provide for loved ones and their future needs. Your estate plan should include provisions for any children, including naming a guardian for children under age 18, and providing for those from a previous marriage who might not be specifically addressed by leaving assets to a current spouse. It also would specifically address the care and income of children or relatives with special needs. This planning must be carefully strategized so as to avoid jeopardizing eligibility for government benefits.

☐ **Protect Your Assets.** A key component of estate planning involves protecting your assets for heirs and your charitable legacy by minimizing expenses and covering estate taxes while still meeting your goals. If necessary, your estate plan would include specific strategies for transferring or disposing of unique assets, such as family-owned business, real estate or investment property, or stock in a closely held business. Many people use permanent life insurance and trusts to protect assets while ensuring future goals can be met. A financial representative can help you find the strategies that best suit your unique situation.

☐ **Document Your Wishes.** If you want your assets distributed in a certain way to meet financial or personal goals, you need to have legal documentation to ensure those wishes are followed if you die or become incapacitated.

This includes designating beneficiaries for your life insurance policies, retirement accounts, and other assets that are in line with your goals, and ensuring that the titles of material assets, such as automobiles and property, are named properly. Work with an attorney to be sure you have an updated will disposing of your assets, a living will that reflects your end-of-life wishes, as well as powers of attorney for health care and financial matters.

☐ **Appoint Fiduciaries.** To execute your estate plan, you must designate someone to act on your behalf if you are unable to do so—as executor of your will, trustee for your assets, legal guardian for your dependents, and/or personal representative or power of attorney if you became incapacitated. You need to be sure your fiduciaries are aware of and agree to their appointments, and that they know where to find your original estate planning documents. Fiduciaries can be family members, personal friends, or hired professionals, such as bankers, attorneys, or corporate trustees. A financial representative can provide more information about trust services and about considering Northwestern Mutual as your trustee.

For more information about these items, visit northwesternmutual.com/financial-guidance/planning-priorities/estate-planning.

Values estate planning checklist:

- ☐ Written letter to spouse/children
- ☐ Family vision statement
- ☐ Favorite memories/stories on video

Extra Credit

Write a letter to your great-great-grandchildren with these as the topics:

- ☐ This is who I was.
- ☐ This is what I believed in.
- ☐ This is what I stood for.
- ☐ This is what I did.
- ☐ This is the difference I hope I made.
- ☐ This is how I hope to be remembered.
- ☐ This is what I really left my children, grandchildren, and you.

Question 4: "Do I have a bridge?"

I loved roller coasters as a kid. My favorite part was going up the first hill. The view from the top was fantastic. I loved seeing the entire amusement park for that brief second or two. But then, down that first immense drop, I felt like I lost my stomach and the ride would never end.

Of course, roller coasters do end, but there comes a point when we stop wanting to remind ourselves that the roller coaster exists. Eventually, they stop feeling fun and start feeling lousy.

The same goes with risk tolerance. I mentioned before how the thinking of clients evolves over time—from invincible to vulnerable. As time passes, clients say they have a greater appreciation for safety and less appreciation for risk. Clients tire of having the performance of their portfolio tied to their happiness (or frustration).

The stock market is like a roller coaster ride, and if this is the only place you have your money invested, you will likely feel those pits in your stomach as the markets hit lows. Yet, we cannot ignore the highs of the stock market either.

The fourth strategy, then, is to build a bridge so that even as you have money invested in the stock market, you have money invested elsewhere so that you will never have to sell your stocks at market lows. Instead, you can use your alternate investments to cover the gap during market lows.

In other words, make sure you have a secondary investment that is not tied to the stock market. This allows you to "ride-out" the lows so that you never have to sell your stocks at market lows.

Build Your Bridge

While we know that historically the market has never been down over more than a 12-year period (during the Great Depression), there have been plenty of big drops in between.

This is not a problem if you do not need the money, but accessing assets for income every year is required in retirement. The secret is to have an alternative asset, uncorrelated to the market, which you can access when needed when the market drops.

In a previous section, we talked about term life insurance earlier. Here, we will talk about the other main type of insurance—permanent life insurance. One of the biggest benefits of permanent life insurance (also called "whole life" or "universal life") is that the cash value cannot go down in value, which makes it a terrific bridge when you need money and your other assets have dropped in value, as they tend to do in aggressive investment vehicles like the stock market.

We advise our clients to strategically accumulate enough cash value in their permanent policies to use during at least three to five years (and ideally ten years), so that they can avoid "selling low" and retain the value of their equity investments for selling when the time is ideal.

As a hypothetical example, if someone retired with $5 million invested in a stock portfolio and liquidated holdings to generate $375,000 of annual income for 25 years taken as a lump sum every year in January, during many market cycles, they would still have $5 million at the end of 25 years.[3]

That sounds pretty good to most people.

However, if they didn't have to sell stocks during the five years when the market was at its lowest, they would end up with $46 million after 25 years.[4]

The nine-fold increase in net worth in this hypothetical scenario was accomplished by strategically funding a cash value life insurance policy that provides sufficient reserves to bridge the down markets.[5]

When do you want to retire and what annual income do you want?

_____

_____

_____

_____

3   S&P 500 Index 1-1-1973 to 12-31-1998. Index is unmanaged and cannot be invested in directly. Standard and Poor's 500 Index® (S&P 500®) is a capitalization-weighted index of 500 stocks. The index is designed to measure performance of the broad domestic economy through changes in the aggregate market value of 500 stocks representing all major industries.
4   S&P 500 Index 1-1-1973 to 12-31-1998 with no withdrawals in 1973, 1974, 1977, 1981 and 1990
5   Utilizing the cash values through policy loans, surrenders, or cash withdrawals will reduce the death benefit; and may necessitate greater outlay than anticipated and/or result in an unexpected taxable event. Assumes a non-Modified Endowment Contract (MEC).

How secure a bridge do you want to build? (In other words, how long do you want to be able to withdraw cash value from your life insurance, without having to sell stock market assets?)

> Typical short market dip = 12 to 18 months
> Average market dip = 24 to 36 months
> Longest market dip = 12 years (Great Depression)

_____

_____

_____

_____

(If you want $200,000 of annual retirement income, and you want to have a bridge to carry you through an average 30-month market dip, then you would need to have at least $500,000 in non-market correlated assets.[6]

Have your financial advisor back into the funding required to build a cash-rich, accumulation oriented life insurance plan so that will have $500,000 of cash value in retirement to weather the market volatility. Multiply your impact to future generations and your favorite charities many times over.)

Another Bridge
Here is another tip: More and more research studies show the value of having some amount of your retirement savings allocated toward assets that provide a guaranteed income for life.

---

6     $500,000 in non-market correlated assets would provide the bridge for 2.5 years of $200,000 retirement income

And keep in mind: 100 is the new 65. More and more studies show that at least one spouse will make it into his or her 100s in the years to come. Of course, Social Security used to help people through the retirement years, but Social Security was implemented when life expectancy was 67. We should not count on Social Security as our saving grace.

And even corporations are doing away with retirement and pension plans. Whereas a pension used to be a standard of a large company, these plans are offered less and less. Instead, employees are expected to manage their own planning.

Many experts are recommending annuities as a replacement for pension plans and supplements to Social Security. These financial instruments provide a guaranteed income for life, no matter how long you live.

Kristi and I have funded annuities for ourselves now so that we can lock in the current life expectancy assumptions, which provide for higher payouts. If future life expectancy tables assume longer lives, then the annuity payouts will likely be proportionately lower.

I recently had lunch with a great client who confided that he wanted to know that he could have a guaranteed income no matter how long he lives. When we showed him that, in fact, this guarantee was already in place through his current plan, he was thrilled.

Question 5: "Have I protected the goose that lays the golden eggs?"

When you were a kid, did you ever stay home from school when you didn't feel well? I'm sure there were a couple days when I faked it and somehow got away with it. As an adult, I don't have the option to fake being sick anymore—especially as an entrepreneur: I don't get paid if I don't show up for work. As a result, I am reluctant to take a sick day.

In fact, I probably average less than one sick day every couple years. When I decide I cannot make it into the office, I truly feel horribly ill. Once we become adults, we do what we have to do because other people are counting on us.

That said, there are some days whereby we cannot handle anything other than recuperating in bed.

Now multiply this feeling by weeks, months, or even 365 days of the year.

I have a dear friend who is a physician who suffers from horrible migraine headaches. When she gets a migraine, she stays in bed with the lights out for days on end. What she describes is more painful than I can imagine enduring. Another buddy started having lower back problems after an injury. He couldn't sit down, couldn't lie down, and found relief only temporarily while walking. Until back surgery, he wasn't able to return to full-time work for nine months.

My point is this: The goose that laid the golden eggs is far, far more valuable than the golden egg itself. As able bodied, working adults, we are that goose. Our ability to earn an income is extraordinarily valuable. Our greatest asset is our future earning potential.

The fifth strategy, then, is to protect your income.

I have had conversations with way too many people who would never think of canceling their home or car insurance, but who have failed to protect their income with disability insurance.

Eventually, my family did recover from that fire. And eventually, I recovered from the three—yes, three!—car accidents that I had during my first three months of living in Los Angeles.

But if I were to become disabled, what would I do? What would my family do?

Unless you are independently wealthy, you should consider obtaining as much long-term disability insurance as you can get—and typically the maximum you can get is 60 percent of your earned income.[7]

My buddy with the excruciating lower back pain? He was not a brick layer or a carpentered. He was a professional speaker.

---

7   The information in the example above may not be representative of the experience of other clients. Disability insurance policies contain exclusions and limitations. The ability to perform the substantial and material duties of your occupation is only one of the factors that determine eligibility for disability benefits and qualification for benefits is determined on a case-by-case basis.

All he really needed was his voice. But when he had pain radiating through his body, he could not even speak. Fortunately, he had sufficient disability coverage, so he was able to use his disability insurance and spend his time recovering.

On the flip side, I have also known people who have had to work through such pain their whole lives because they did not have the option. Thank goodness this wasn't the case for my friend.

Assuming you currently have good health, you can eliminate this risk for yourself and your family, too.

If disability insurance still seems unimportant, think of it like this: Imagine that you are given two job offers for identical jobs, but with two different compensation packages.

- Job A pays you 98 percent when you are healthy, and 60 percent if you cannot work.
- Job B pays you 100 percent when you are healthy and able to work, but nothing if you are sick or get disabled.

Almost no one would pick Job B.

Yet, if you do not purchase disability insurance, you are essentially choosing Job B. (A great disability plan costs about two percent of your income.) The reality is, if you think it would be hard getting by on 60 percent, then it would certainly be hard getting by with no income whatsoever.

For those who are young and healthy, it's hard to envision a sickness or injury interrupting your ability to earn a living.

Smart Money • Section 1

But one of every four employees will be disabled for three months or more at some point during their career (U.S. Social Security Administration, Fact Sheet February 7, 2013).

If your employer offers a comprehensive package of benefits, you may have access to group disability income insurance at work. Most group plans cover short-term disability (typically six months to two years) and may also include long-term disability. And that's a great starting point.

But it may not be enough, because most group plans:

- Cover only a portion of your base income (typically 50-60 percent).
- Deliver benefits that are usually subject to income tax.
- End when you leave the company.

Remember, I want you to protect the goose that lays the golden eggs: You!

To further protect yourself and others who rely on your income, you may want to consider supplementing your group coverage with individual long-term disability insurance.

Individual long-term disability insurance helps close the gap between what is covered by your employer's group policy and your monthly take-home pay. If a disability were to keep you from working, the coverage provided by a supplemental individual insurance policy will help you:

Disability Insurance policies contain exclusions and limitations that could affect individual coverage.

- **Better maintain your current standard of living.** You will worry less about keeping up with your bills or making sacrifices, like giving up your gym membership or canceling piano lessons for the kids. (Plus, if you pay policy premiums with after-tax dollars, benefits will be paid to you, income-tax free.)

- **Minimize the impact on your long-term financial security.** You will lower the need to tap into your savings—or worse yet, your retirement savings—to meet expenses during a time of disability.

Key considerations for protecting your income:

What's the longest vacation you could afford to take? *If it's not forever, then you probably would benefit from long-term disability insurance.*	
Do you have any group long-term disability insurance from your employer?	
Does the company pay for it? *If so, that typically means that the benefits are taxable as ordinary income.*	

Explore supplemental disability insurance with your financial planning professional as soon as possible. During our working years we are many more times as likely to become disabled than as to die.

Question 6: "Have I considered long-term care?"

At about the same time, both of my grandmas started for-getting things. They were each in fine physical health, living on their own, and loving their independence well into their eighties.

However, sometimes they forgot to take their medicine, or they forgot the last time they ate.

Obviously, we took action as soon as we noticed that they needed additional assistance, but our strategies differed because my grandmothers had varied financial situations.

They both wanted to stay in their homes, but only one of them had been prudent with her money. My grandmother who had planned for and considered long-term care was able to afford the care we wanted her to have, so she was able to stay in her home, with the help of an aide who came daily.

She continued to lead a life with great dignity and it showed in her attitude and demeanor.

My other grandma didn't have any savings. She ended up moving in with my mom. While my mom wouldn't have had it any other way, I saw what a burden it was on her. She had gotten her nursing license by then, but if you have ever been a caregiver, you know how difficult it is to be responsi-ble for every imaginable need for another human being, es-pecially your parent. (Like I said earlier, my mom is an angel!)

Sadly, even my grandma who started off with money ended up spending the vast majority of it on her long-term care. They had both wanted to leave an inheritance to their children and grandchildren, but after funding their long-term care needs, their resources were exhausted.

In seeing this happen with my grandmothers, I quickly realized that I was my parents' long-term-care plan. They didn't have the money to provide for their end-of-life needs. I was certainly going to do whatever it took to take care of them, just as they had done for their mothers.

Thankfully, we were able to successfully do the appropriate planning to ensure their needs would be met if a future long-term care event were to occur.

Going through this experience was awakening to Kristi and me. We felt that this was important planning for us and our family to jump start sooner rather than later. Although we are still relatively young, it gives us great piece of mind to know that we've put the correct pieces in place to ensure our family needs will be met and our retirement will maintain its course.

I have seen many families torn apart by the squabbles that come from deciding how inheritance dollars should be used. If someone has been counting on money coming their way, it can be hard to see it eroded by the ever-increasing cost of providing health care out-of-pocket and with after-tax dollars. I am glad to have all these costs paid for in advance. I want my kids to focus on taking great care of me and supporting each other during my final years.

29%
of adult U.S
population

Fewer than a third have addressed the need for long-term care within their own retirement plans.

Source: Northwestern Mutual's
2014 Long-Term Care Study

Having a plan in place in the event of a long-term-care event may be one of the most important steps you can take to help ensure your future financial security. And yet, it is the one area of financial planning that often goes unaddressed.

There are many reasons why people don't make planning for long-term care a priority.

- It's difficult to think about.

No one wants to consider the possibility that they or a loved one may someday experience the need for long-term care as a result of a debilitating illness from a disease like Multiple Sclerosis, a cognitive impairment such as dementia, or the results of an accident like paralysis.

- It's difficult to talk about.

In a recent Northwestern Mutual study, 35 percent of people said talking to their parents about long-term care would be one of the most difficult conversations they could possibly have—right up there with asking them to borrow money or asking their boss for a raise.

- Young people believe they are invincible.

Many people think long-term care is something that only the elderly need worry about, yet an accident or debilitating illness can strike at any time.

- It happens only to someone else.
- They think Medicare covers it.

Key considerations for long-term care:

If you live to the age of 65, there's a 70 percent chance you will eventually need some kind of long-term care.[2]

Would you prefer self-funding or "ear-marking" $1 million of accumulated retirement assets to fund future long-term care needs or shifting the risk by doing proactive planning?[3]

Morningstar reports that 78 percent in need of long-term care who receive that care from family members and friends.

2   http://beta.latimes.com/business/la-fi-retirement-long-term-care-20171116-story.html
3   http://news.morningstar.com/articlenet/article.aspx?id=564139

Many people mistakenly believe that if something happens, the cost of long-term care will be covered by Medicare, Medicaid or private health insurance. Most often it won't, which is why people need to have a plan in place for how they would manage such expenses.

For all of these reasons, a long-term care event can have a significant impact on you and your family—financially, physically and emotionally. That's why it's important to plan for long-term care.

Question 7: "To enjoy its shade, when was the best day to plant a tree?"

The answer is: Twenty years ago.

This advice applies not only to planting trees, but also to planning your children's education. The best time to plant the seed for their education is well before they need it.

That said, experts say that college students with "skin in the game" spend less money during college, finish college sooner, and get better grades.

I worked two jobs to pay my way through college, and I don't want this for my kids. I do, however, want them to spend less money, get better grades, and graduate in four or fewer years.

How can I accomplish this?

There are many ways to fund a college education and the advantages/disadvantages of each should be discussed with your financial professional. I've made a deal with my kids that I'll give them what I call a "Personal Responsibility Account." I will fund their PRA through college. Instead of having to take loans to pay for school, they'll borrow from themselves through their PRA. When they graduate from college, they will take over the annual funding of the PRA, as well as pay themselves back from the money they borrowed from the PRA.

45

The mechanism I am using to fund the PRA is a permanent life insurance policy on each child. The kids have already begun to appreciate how fast the cash value is growing in the life insurance policy for their future benefit.

We started their plans at birth. In other words, we planted the seeds, and watching the accounts compound over time has been extraordinary. We have given them a gift they could never recreate on their own. This is something I wish my parents had done for me, so I'm thrilled to provide this for my children.

Our deal is that as long as they are good kids, working hard in school and maturing as responsible citizens, then we will give them all the cash value as part of the life insurance, which they can take over funding after graduating from college. At the same time, they know that if they do not become contributing members of society, their mom and I will cash out the plans and take a fantastic vacation!

Plant the seed of this amazing tool for them now so that they can enjoy the benefits and protection from its "shade" for decades and decades to come.

Remember, the best day to plant a tree was twenty years ago. Our kids are too young to plant it for themselves, but we can plant it for them now—and they'll always remember you for it.

Questions to consider in planning gifts to children:

Did you get an inheritance? Was it financial, wisdom, and/or experiences?

_____

_____

_____

_____

Do you want to give your kids a head start? If so, how?

_____

_____

_____

_____

When did you start your first meaningful savings plan?

_____

_____

_____

Would you have liked to have started saving earlier?

_____

_____

_____

Question 8: "Would you bet on the horse that has a fancy name and looks good, or the one that won 76 of the last 86 races?"

Year after year, other companies (that are for the most part investing in the same market) regularly project higher performance, but over the last 86 years, Northwestern Mutual has led the industry 76 times, including every one of the last 36 years.[8]

While I cannot guarantee how Northwestern will perform going forward, only three factors impact cash value performance, and Northwestern excels at each.

First, while a company's investment returns might fluctuate from year to year, there is a regression to the mean over time. In other words, one company might have a great year, but over time, most companies average performance gets closer and closer because they are for the most part investing in the same market.

The final factors—expenses and mortality costs—take decades to materially change. Northwestern has led in these categories year after year, a lot of which can be attributed to very rigorous underwriting and having headquarters in much less expensive Milwaukee, WI, instead of New York City or Boston.

---

8   Source: 20 year policy performance data for a Male age 45. Flitcraft Compend (1927-1967), Best's Flitcraft Compend (1968-1994), Best's Policy Reports (1995-2000), Full Disclosure (2002-2013). Surrender Cost Index calculated by Northwestern Mutual from 1927- 1981. No published data for 2001. New York Life did not participate in 1927, 1999 and 2000. MassMutual did not participate in 1988. Based on S&P Global data.

The "76/86" referred to in the title was based on the surrender cost index, which is the measure of policy performance and cost of ownership. Northwestern Mutual has been first on this measure all but ten times:

- In 1972 and 1973—New York Life outranked Northwestern Mutual (policies issued in 1952 and 1953)
- From 1993 through 2000—Guardian Life outranked Northwestern Mutual (policies issued 1973 – 1980)

Based on this, you could say that Northwestern Mutual has outperformed the competition consistently since 1981. When you consider that during its years as #2, it was outranked by only one company, Northwestern's track record is remarkable.

Here are some other statistics from the past 21 years (1996-2016) among Northwestern Mutual and it's closest competitors (New York Life, Mass Mutual, Guardian, Penn Mutual, and Ohio National):

- None of the above had better expense ratios than Northwestern Mutual
- Only one company in one year (Penn Mutual, 2016) had a better lapse ratio than Northwestern Mutual
- None had a better mortality margin ratio than Northwestern Mutual

S&P Global Market Intelligence, our primary data source for this, provides statutory financial data back to 1996, so we cannot provide a definitive "how long" for any of these measures—but this is long enough to show extraordinary consistency.[9] The industry standard statistics were calculated by the Northwestern Mutual home office using this data.

---

9   Source: 20 year policy performance data for a Male age 45. Flitcraft Compend (1927-1967), Best's Flitcraft Compend (1968-1994), Best's Policy Reports (1995-2000), Full Disclosure (2002-2013). Surrender Cost Index calculated by Northwestern Mutual from 1927- 1981. No published data for 2001. New York Life did not participate in 1927, 1999 and 2000. MassMutual did not participate in 1988.

Many companies in the life insurance industry point to their illustrations as evidence of superior performance. Many claim that they are better positioned for the future. However, historically, no matter how good its competitors' illustrations may have looked or what silver bullet they may have claimed to have found, they have had little success when it comes to matching Northwestern Mutual's actual policy performance.

Northwestern Mutual's strong performance in the areas of mortality experience and expense management, beyond its solid investment performance, have allowed Northwestern Mutual to consistently provide superior actual long-term value to their policy owners.

For all these reasons, Kristi and I put half of our long-term savings into our retirement plans invested in equities and the other half as premiums into Northwestern Mutual permanent life insurance, representing those safer dollars that we value more and more.

My wife loves this consistent, tax-advantaged performance year after year, and so do my clients.

Smart Money Scorecard
Score Yourself from 1-12

Mindsets	1	2	3	4	5	6
Excitement for a Bigger Future	You feel isolated from a rapidly changing world and are in conflict internally with what you want and the small future you fear is yours.			You are searching for ways to create a bigger future and find your current way of doing things to be exhausting and want a better path.		
The Role of Life Insurance	You see insurance as a waste of money and would rather self insure.			You love your family and want to provide for them, but haven't yet addressed the role of life insurance.		
The Value of Estate Planning	You haven't seen value in planning and expect your kids to figure it out for themselves.			You have been meaning to get a will and trust in place, but you always seem to be too busy.		
Bridging for Your Success	You are happy when your portfolio is up and depressed when it goes down. It's essential that your plan always beats the stock market.			You have been disappointed by the market historically and want a plan that gets you to the finish line without tremendous effort/stress.		
Are You the Golden Goose?	You feel that you could do your job from the hospital bed if need be. Buying disability insurance is a bad bet.			You don't know how disability insurance works or how much you have, but you would want to protect your future earning potential.		
The Role of Long-Term Care	You have no interest in long-term-care protection.			You are open to learning more about mitigating the significant risk that a long-term-care event poses to your retirement goals.		
Investing for Your Children	You started out with nothing and you don't want to handicap your children with assets that could potentially disincentivize them.			You haven't spent much time on ways to leverage gifts to your kids but you'd like to give them advantages that incentivize them.		
The Importance of Quality & Track Record	You don't trust others to help you in your planning. You prefer to do everything yourself and live with your choices.			You don't want to take risks on products & services just because they are cheapest. You want a plan and partners that deliver tested value.		
Scorecard	➡	➡	➡	➡	➡	➡

For recommendations on reaching your goals, complete this scorecard online at smartmoney.vip

						Current Score	Desired Score
7	**8**	**9**	**10**	**11**	**12**		
You feel settled where you are, and because of your credentials and community respect, you are already at the top of your game.			Your future is expanding exponentially and your choices today create a future surpassing what was previously possible.				
You have addressed all your life insurance needs and aren't looking for any additional advice.			You are always looking for new strategies to leverage your current and future legacy planning.				
You have utilized the best estate planning resources and are confident that everything is addressed.			You recognize that no one has cornered the market on good ideas and welcome new insights to pass on your values to prepare your children.				
You have got an incredible team of advisors who take great care of you.			You value bridges in your portfolio that protect you from selling during market lows and provide income for life.				
You have maxed out your group insurance and purchased as much supplemental disability protection as possible.			You know your greatest asset is the income you are yet to earn and want to do everything possible to protect it for you and your family.				
You have self-insured or bought all the long-term-care insurance you want and feel confident that this isn't an issue for you.			You want to make sure that you and your loved ones never have to choose between quality health care and quality of life. LTC is essential.				
You feel good about the gifting you have done for your family and plan to spend the rest on the future you've earned.			You are raising responsible children and, within reasonable limits, you want to leverage every opportunity to support their best future.				
You have exhaustively searched the market for the best financial planning resources and have everything in place for your future.			You never skimp on quality and proven historical results. You welcome ways to increase the confidence you desire for your family and their best future.				

Section 2

8 Mindsets to Enjoy Your Life by Design

Taking action is important, but so too is making sure that your mindset is pointed toward your biggest future. Here are eight mindsets you can explore to best advance yourself to a life of your design.

1. Find Your Passion and Do What You Love Using Your Unique Ability®

Dan Sullivan, founder of Strategic Coach®, spends much time with his clients discussing their Unique Ability®, a phrase he coined to describe that unique combination of talent and passion that reflects not only what a person loves to do, but also what he is good at doing. Since Sullivan has introduced the concept, it has spread like wildfire, launching countless entrepreneurs to higher levels of achievement.

This section provides a brief explanation of the Unique Ability®, but to truly understand and capitalize on your own Unique Ability®, sign up for Strategic Coach® (strategiccoach.com) or read *Unique Ability* by Catherine Nomura.

The purpose of the Unique Ability® is to pinpoint and under-stand that specific component of your being that allows you to achieve your biggest results and, at the same time, reach fulfillment, thereby providing you with a balanced life.

1. What are you best at?
2. What are you exceptionally skilled at doing,

considering your attitude, energy and enthusiasm?
3. What are your strengths and when do you shine?
4. What is the single attribute that most accurately describes you?
5. What single activity would keep you absolutely fascinated and motivated for the rest of your life?

When you have clarity on the answers to questions, you will begin to understand your Unique Ability®.

Yet, it is not enough to ask those questions yourself. To understand your Unique Ability®, you will need to broaden your perspective and seek insight from your friends, family, and co-workers to discover what it is that they believe drives you. When you see yourself in a mirror or a photograph, much of the depth, color, and layers go unseen. You see only one side of the picture.

The same principle applies when evaluating your strengths, weaknesses, and contribution to the world. Another person's experience of you will undoubtedly be subtly different than your own, and will help you gain a fuller picture of your abilities.

Gaining this insight allows you to see sides of you that are present in every relationship, which leads to a greater understanding of what drives you.

By working with Dan Sullivan and reading *Unique Ability*®, I was able to narrow my Unique Ability® to the following: "My Unique Ability® is meeting, befriending, and connecting people to help them create bigger futures, reaching their most amazing future sooner than anyone expects."

What about you? Begin asking your closest friends, family members, colleagues, or clients these questions, and record their answers. Look for commonalities and through lines.

1. What am I best at?

_____

_____

2. What I am exceptionally skilled at doing, considering my attitude, energy and enthusiasm?

_____

_____

3. What are my strengths and when do I shine?

_____

_____

4. What is the attribute that most accurately describes me?

_____

_____

5. What single activity would keep me absolutely fascinated and motivated for the rest of my life?

_____

_____

2. Work Hard: The 1869 Secret to Success

Angela Duckworth tells this story in her book *Grit*: Francis Galton was Charles Darwin's cousin, and by all accounts, he was a child prodigy. He could read and write by four, and by six, he knew Latin, long division, and Shakespeare, which he could recite. Duckwroth writes this:

> **Ability, zeal, and a capacity for hard labor: These are the secrets to high achievement.**

"In 1869, Galton published his first scientific study on the origins of high achievement. After assembling lists of well-known figures in science, athletics, music, poetry, and law—among other domains—he gathered whatever biographical information he could. Outliers, Galton concluded, are remarkable in three ways: they demonstrate unusual 'ability' in combination with exceptional 'zeal' and 'the capacity for hard labor.'"

Ability, zeal, and a capacity for hard labor: These are the secrets to high achievement.

When you identify your Unique Ability®, you can naturally address ability and zeal, but working hard is the essential third part of the equation.

That said, working hard is a lot easier when you are in your zone—when you are using your Unique Ability®. I love Dan Sullivan's encouragement to identify the single focus and activity that will keep you absolutely fascinated and motivated for the rest of your life.

When we work hard at this, it's not so hard after all—and the results are most often extraordinary.

3. Think Big and Outside the Box

My dear friend Will Richardson and I happened to find ourselves in Milwaukee on January 9. We both love running, so we decided to go for an early morning 10K. It was 10 degrees and dark along Lake Michigan when we came up with the idea to launch a "Gathering of Titans" event to provide more opportunities for our most successful associates to learn from each other and grow together.

We had no real idea where this "Gathering of Titans" event would go. We were brainstorming during a chilly run, but we thought it could be fun.

More than 200 of Northwestern's top advisors will be there, investing their time and money to take their growth to the next level.

The Titans idea is intended to provide a curriculum for sharing best practices and collaborating with like-minded peers who want to reach their most amazing future sooner than anyone expects.

My point is this: We all have hare-brained ideas that might actually have a chance at changing the world. Write them down, share them with trusted friends, and see what's possible when you think big and outside the box.

What's a hare-brained idea that you think might change the world?

_____

_____

_____

_____

_____

_____

_____

_____

_____

_____

_____

_____

_____

_____

_____

_____

_____

_____

_____

4. Be Curious and Open Minded

So much of the excitement I feel on a daily basis comes from staying curious about what is going on, what is possible, and who can I learn from.

When things are not going your way, it is easy to close down, blame others, and feel out of control. But, if you stay curious about what you can learn from the situation and remind yourself to be constructive, you can gain wisdom. You will know how to approach things differently the next time around.

The biggest victories often come after catastrophic failures, but if we do not stay curious and open minded to the lessons from those failures, it can be easy to miss opportunities for growth.

We know the people at the top of their game struggled, put in effort, and overcame a lot of challenges, but it is easy to think they arrived at success through natural talent and little effort. And, we can use that erroneous thinking as an excuse for why we should not even try to overcome setbacks. After long, frustrating efforts without the results for which we have been hoping, we can simply say we are not cut out for success.

This mindset, though, will not invite success. Instead, stay curious. Ask how a bad experience can be fuel for ingeniously. How can your failures make you wiser?

I enjoy making a game of challenging circumstances. This is what I do: When something goes wrong, I challenge myself to see what is now possible as a result of the detour.

This open mindedness makes all the difference between the victim versus victor approach to life. I regularly find that there are strategic byproducts that could only have come from being in the place I had not planned to go.

5. Leverage the Genius of Others

When I'm stuck, I not only look for ways that my roadblocks can become a catalyst for growth, but I also look for others from whom I can learn.

It's often only in the midst of difficulty that we explore the resources around us to find solutions and opportunities for growth, but leveraging the genius of others is always important. It is not just helpful in times of difficulty. It is often the secret to breakthroughs.

In the past year, I have dealt with the loss of family members, the failure of dreams and the disappointment of plans that went awry. In each situation, there's the easy option to play the victim or the decision to make the most of every circumstance. It's always through reaching out to dear friends that I'm reminded of what's most important who also provide clarity to get through the storm. Steve Reasner has been by my side almost every day of my life in Los Angeles. Michelle Menees has been a rock of solace since college. Ethan Frey texts me every morning with his favorite verse from that day's Bible reading.

I have been so inspired by Robert Cooper (cooperstrategic. com), Peter Diamandis and his Abundance 360 community (a360.digital) and Dan Sullivan's Strategic Coach program (strategiccoach.com). Their podcasts and so many others are a readily available treasure chest of wisdom for us to explore and integrate.

I love the proverb that if you want to go fast, go alone, but if you want to go far, go with others. Despite my default desire to go fast, I can't forget to leverage the genius of all the amazing people around me.

Let's go far together!

Who can I learn from within my network?

_____

_____

_____

_____

_____

_____

_____

_____

_____

_____

_____

_____

_____

_____

_____

_____

6. Be Transparent and Ask for Help

One of the hardest things for me to do is ask for help. I don't like admitting that I am not self-sufficient. I fear that others will think less of me if I ask for their support.

Yet, what I have found over and over is that the more transparent I am, the more people rally around me. We are naturally inclined to reach out to those in need and, in fact, we feel really good after making a contribution to another that helps them move forward in life.

Not so long ago, I was working hard to reach a goal in business. A dear friend and mentor of mine asked me how things were going as I headed into the final days of this particular initiative. The truth was that I had next to no time and absolutely zero idea how I would reach my goal.

I hesitated to share this, but his heartfelt request to know of my progress softened my mask of self-sufficiency. I shared where I was: It didn't look like I would accomplish my objective.

Without saying a word in response, my friend and mentor (who also happens to be a client) called his assistant into the room.

"Please bring me my checkbook," he said.

Since my friend's financial plan showed that he had need for additional life insurance, he decided to write a check for the additional coverage right then and there.

I was blown away.

"You don't need to do this," I said to my friend, who already has a sizeable amount of money invested with me.

"Yes," he said, "I do. I have been wanting to add to my portfolio for a while, but I have not gotten around to it. Helping you meet your goal is the extra push I needed."

I'll never forget the incredible generosity of my friend. The ripples of his gesture have caused me to look for ways to be extraordinarily generous whenever I can, and I always feel wonderful when I do have a chance to help others.

It reminds me to ask, and you should do the same. When you ask someone for help, you are giving them the opportunity to support you, which always feels good to them.

7. Accountability

My alarm clock sounds at 4:40 a.m. on most every Tuesday and Thursday so I can exercise at the beach with my work-out partner, Juan Baron. I love exercising at the beach, but meeting at 5:30 a.m. isn't my first preference. Yet, it's the best time of day for Juan, and I place a high priority on this time with him. With Juan as an accountability partner, I do far more than I would ever do on my own.

Who are your accountability partners?

Having an accountability partner has several benefits. First, we often feel more committed to other people than we do to ourselves. I would likely skip a few morning workouts were it not for Juan, but knowing that he is also rising from his bed at 4:40 a.m. prevents me from pushing that snooze button.

It also gives our brain more evidence that we are committed to our goals. When multiple people are in the same corner, all working toward the same goal, we are more likely to achieve our goals than if we simply store them in our brains.

The third way it helps is by reminding me to maintain a posi-tive attitude. My partners and I have this rule: One of us can be in a bad mood, but never both of us. This rule forces me to let the small things go so that I can be there if my partner is having a bad day. It's always our responsibility to be there for our friends (and vice versa), and, in doing so, we end up helping ourselves, too.

Here are a few other ways I have used accountability partners:

1. I have a "personal board of advisors" to whom I send weekly emails detailing the breakthroughs that I'm testing in various areas of my life. I have been sending this weekly email for 428 weeks now, and to be certain, there were plenty of weeks when I did not particularly feel likely spilling my soul and identifying new ways to get better.

   Yet, I hold myself accountable to continue my personal growth to these people who mean so much to me. After eight years of weekly breakthrough testing, it's become a habit that I don't see myself stopping in the foreseeable future. It continues on those weeks when I would rather be doing something else because of my accountability team.

2. Tomorrow, I am meeting with another accountability team, aptly called my "accountability group." For more than 20 years, we have been meeting every quarter to share our goals and track our results. These amazing men have walked beside me through great times and very difficult times, and I have continued to be inspired and to grow because of them.

   On plenty of occasions, I have been in the dumps and wondered if things were ever going to turn around. Every time, things got better through the help of my accountability group. When we're in a funk, it's easy to stay there and fall into the self-fulfilling prophecy of "woe is me," but when we call on accountability partners, they remind us to call our best selves forward, and to work our way out of our frustrations.

3. In addition to having accountability partners who lift me up, I always offer accountability and mentorship to young advisors. I just returned from a speech in New York where, over dinner, I had the pleasure of sitting next to a young advisor who had been the winningest college wrestler in United States history. Yet, he was not having all the success he wanted in this new venture. I shared some of my story: Given Northwestern Mutual's current performance standards, I would have been fired many times over at the start to my financial planning career.

    The fact that I survived, and ultimately thrived, is what makes my story even more encouraging to new advisors, including this young gentleman.

    I challenged him to make a move that would propel him forward to even greater success. He wrote down his new commitment, and then added why it was so important to him and his family.

    To help him be accountable, we took a picture of him holding up his commitment and why it was important. He shared it with his accountability partner from his office who will post it and remind him to stay after his bigger goals and the actions to make them real.

8. Have Faith

The fundamental secret to my success has been to have faith through it all. As a man of Christian faith, I have always been able to turn to the Bible, my friends, and my pastors for the support and encouragement I need in the most desperate times.

I have two buddies who also start each day by reading the Bible. For almost two years now, we have texted each other the Bible verse that meant the most to us from that morning's reading and turned it into an identity statement. Just yesterday, I shared 2 Corinthians 5:7: "We live by faith, not by sight."

My identity statement was, "I am living by faith and loving the adventure of trusting Him through this wild and unpredictable world."

You can just imagine the wonderful influence of seeing more than 1,000 of these affirmations throughout the year pop onto my phone each morning.

For me, growing in faith is a daily journey, and I am regularly tested, but by surrounding myself with people who care about me, I continue to grow through the best and worst of times.

What can you do to feed your faith and continue to grow with greater confidence?

_____

_____

_____

_____

_____

_____

_____

_____

_____

_____

_____

_____

_____

_____

_____

_____

_____

_____

_____

_____

Your Life by Design

Score Yourself from 1-12

Mindsets	1	2	3	4	5	6
Unique Ability	You feel that there are required tasks that drain your energy and only you can do them.			You spend much of your time on mundane activities but hope for that to change over time.		
Work Hard	You know that others work hard, but you're not willing to sacrifice your free time to get ahead.			You are willing to work as hard as anyone else, but wish that you were making more progress toward your most important goals.		
Think Big and Outside the Box	You find it hard to focus on the big picture and are frightened that you may be taken advantage of somehow by missing a detail.			You want to think bigger for your future but aren't sure where to start or how to make it real.		
Curious and Open Minded	You feel that you're on a path that is essentially outside your control and aren't motivated to explore options.			You would like to be more curious and open minded but have struggled so much just to get where you are.		
Leverage the Genius of Others	You can't imagine that you can learn much from others and prefer to double down on yourself.			You are encouraged by the things you learn from others and are beginning to look for others to support your goals.		
Transparency and Asking for Help	You fear the risk of sharing your needs and would never ask others for help.			You can see how others could help you, but you don't know how to ask in a way that "saves face."		
Accountability	You like to focus on your own path, and you don't need others to tell you what to do.			You haven't had empowering mentors, but you believe that inspiring partners could raise your game.		
Have Faith	You don't rely on anyone but yourself, and that's just fine.			You believe that we're more than just primordial sludge, and you'd like to access more confidence with additional "spiritual" clarity.		
Scorecard	⇨	⇨	⇨	⇨	⇨	⇨

Current Score	Desired Score

7	8	9	10	11	12		
You are satisfied with your daily activities and don't see a need to improve things.			You are spending more and more time doing just the activities that give energy and provide never ending opportunities for growth.				
You are recognized for your hard work and take pride in the hours you put in even though it's crowding out other priorities.			You focus on projects that will keep you absolutely fascinated and motivated for the rest of your life. This hard work is fun.				
You have been rewarded by seeing the big picture in some instances, though you find yourself complacent regarding new risks.			You have great confidence that your best decisions come from understanding the big picture and getting ingenious to reach your top goals.				
You have been open minded about most things and hope that everything continues to go well for you.			You believe that you can learn and grow from every circumstance; setbacks are opportunities for breakthroughs.				
You are admired by others and like learning from others to a point, though you often wonder what is left for you to learn.			You are constantly curious to learn from others with different capabilities and love the idea of leveraging the genius of others.				
You will ask for help as needed, but still prefer to maintain the image that you've got it all together.			You readily share your needs and see that as a strength to get the support you need and encourage similar transparency for others.				
You have a great accountability team and you don't need anyone else to support your success.			You are always looking for new ways to engage others to raise your game and reach maximum potential.				
You have faith in yourself and in a higher power and are content with where you are.			You are empowered by your faith and it's an ever-more important part of who you are and who you are becoming.				

Section 3
8 Hallmarks of Wisdom for Empowering the Next Generation

Years ago, while attending a seminar, the keynote speaker at the event selected me from the crowd and asked me to share the names of my great-grandparents. I could not name one of them. I was mortified.

While my initial reaction was sheer embarrassment, before long. it became frustration and concern that my great-grandchildren might not know my name. Would Vyvien, Jordan, or Christian's grandchildren not know my name? This possibility deeply affected me.

It seemed impossible considering how much grandparents dote on their grandkids, the intense love, commitment, and obligation they feel for them, and the effectual contribution they make to their lives. Yet, in asking this question to colleagues and clients, I have learned that I am not alone in being unable to recollect the names of relatives I think I should know.

The reality is that unless you do something really good or really bad, your family will forget you in three generations, or about 88 years. In less than a century, the odds are that your great-grandchildren will not know your name, much less what you stood for or what your hopes and dreams were for them.

You might say, "Wait a minute! My future generations will inherit my wealth and they will remember me for that!" But passing on only money to future generations is not enough.

In working with over 2,000 clients, I have come to realize that families who are tight-knit and who last the test of time tend to share the same traits—namely, they have tools for passing along not only their money but also their wisdom and values.

Too many people think of a legacy as an inheritance—something they leave behind after they die. Yet, much more important than the tools you use for transferring money is the importance of planning, documenting, and sharing personal values and goals as a way to give your great-grandchildren something to inspire and guide them as well as remember you by.

Here are eight strategies for empowering the next generation and building close family bonds so that you leave behind a legacy.

1. Expand Your Definition of Wealth

Families who successfully use wealth as a vehicle to protecting and supporting the family have a different definition of wealth that extends well beyond money. As related to the idea of using wealth for security, success, and significance, consider expanding your definition of wealth, as described by Jay Hughes, author of *Family Wealth: Keeping It in the Family.*

- Human Capital is comprised of your family, health, backgrounds, talents, and attitudes.

- Intellectual Capital includes formal and informal education, work ethic, spiritual life, family stories, and life lessons.

- Social Capital includes citizenship, philanthropy, and volunteer work.

- Financial Capital includes the traditional definition of wealth—all of your personal property and assets.

We usually know how to pass along financial wealth, but we must also pass along emotional wealth, which is the sum total of values, life lessons, stories, and experiences we have discussed.

If we don't understand our emotional inheritance, we cannot protect our human capital, our intellectual capital, or our social capital. As a result, our financial wealth will die. It is, after all, a byproduct of human capital, intellectual capital, and social capital.

When you consider, then, all four of these capitals in your definition of wealth, you begin to see that you must have a plan in place to protect and transfer your emotional wealth as well.

It starts by identifying your values.

2. Identify Your Values

My inability to recall the names of my great-grandparents coupled with the birth of my first child prompted me to create the Estes Family Tree Legacy, a 188-year plan for transferring the values I want to pass on to future Estes generations. The first part of the plan identifies the values I want to pass along to my children, grandchildren, and great-grandchildren.

These are:

- Christian faith and evangelism
- Love of family
- Educational excellence
- Charity
- Entrepreneurship
- Goal setting and personal growth
- Community service
- Carpe Diem—Having fun while seizing the day

At the same time, I recognize that everyone of us is different, and I want to embrace the individuality of my children and future generations. We each are blessed with special gifts, and I encourage everyone to become the best version of themselves and to add their unique passions and values to continue accelerating the positive impact we can make for our world.

Now is the time to begin working on your Family Tree Legacy™, even if your children are grown. Start with identifying the values you want to pass on to your family, such as faith, education, charity, entrepreneurship, goal setting, or community involvement.

What about you? What values do you want to pass along to future generations?

_____

_____

_____

_____

_____

_____

_____

_____

_____

_____

_____

_____

_____

_____

_____

_____

_____

3. Identify the Tools, Vehicles, or Incentives for Passing Along These Values.

The next part of my legacy is to create the tools and vehicles for transferring these values. If I want my great-grandchildren to attend my alma mater, for instance, I can create an incentive through endowments and scholarships.

Here are a few of my other incentives used to encourage future generations to appreciate my values:

- Education funded 100 percent for pre-school through bachelor of science degree.
- $10,000 a year (increased with inflation) personal improvement grant for a Strategic Coach®-type program. Access to a matched earning fund up to $100,000 a year. If they are a teacher or in the ministry, they will receive $2 for every $1 that they earn, or if they are an entrepreneur they will receive $1 for every $2 that they earn.
- $1,000 a day for up to 10 days per year spent doing charitable work, encouraging them to donate the money back to the organization.
- $1 million Northwestern Mutual life insurance policy funded for them from birth through college.
- Upon their graduation from college, on their birthday every year, I will fund a long weekend at the Four Seasons or equivalent resort to ensure that they remember me most fondly!

Here are some of the tools I am using to pass on these values:

- Set aside $5 million for our family's education using a dynasty trust.
- Set aside $5 million for the capitalism-matching fund for future generations.
- Establish $100,000 written goal reward/encouragement fund.
- Set aside $10 million for the Estes Family Foundation making four percent annual grants with children's involvement in selecting the charities and, ideally, participation with the recipient organizations.

What incentives, vehicles, and tools will you use to pass along the values you identified on the previous worksheet?

_____

_____

_____

_____

_____

_____

_____

_____

_____

_____

Bonus: go to www.smartmoney.vip to see the brilliant ideas of others including the "Meaning Fund" tuition application that David Adams put in place to help his grandchildren make the most of their high school experience.

4. Family Fun, Family Development, and Family Business Transactions

Your values, your wealth, and your tradition can be transferred only if your family is unified. Do they have shared memories? Do they have shared interests? Are they committed to growing together?

Perry Cochell and Rod Zeeb, authors of *Beating the Midas Curse*, have identified this strategy: Intentionally create bonds of history and experience through fun, development, and enrichment.

Family Fun: What can you do to create shared memories as a family? This includes vacations, attending sporting events, or playing games. As your family grows and changes, so too will these activities. It matters not what the activities are, or how they change, so long as they can be shared by the entire family.

Family Development: How can you develop the knowledge of your family base? Perhaps you can read books together, attend speaking engagements, or visit museums. Again, the possibilities vary based on your family's unique constellation of traits, interests, strengths, and weaknesses.

Family Business Transactions: Families with longevity often undertake business activities, which are separate and distinct from any business or investments the family may own. These business transactions are intended to inspire individual family members and build family unity and a common family vision.

You might, for instance, help your young children build their financial acumen by making hats that can be sold at a local farmer's market. You might work with your grandchildren to fund a charity. Our family trip to Mexico where we built a house was an example of the family partaking in a business experience together for the sake of the family.

When you engage in business transactions with your family, conversations will open up. You will have the ability to talk to your children about money, values, decisions, and justice. Children will get to see their parents involved in some activities as equal participants, not as facilitators or leaders.

What can you do with your family?
Write your ideas below.

Family Fun:

_____

_____

Family Development:

_____

_____

Family Business Transactions:

_____

_____

5. Training and Mentoring Future Generations

Mentoring for success is a hallmark characteristic of families who successfully sustain their wealth and unity. After all, intellectual capital is one component of wealth. If it is ignored, financial capital will likely begin to erode. Your commitment to this has the ability to change future generations from frightfully entitled to inspirationally empowered.

Mentoring can take place in many arenas. It includes expanding business acumen and teaching children to invest and protect money. It might include real-work skills. And it might include the mentoring of values. Children can, for instance, learn about the power of giving. They can learn how and why their parents have selected the charitable organizations they support and the difference their giving has made in the world.

I call these "pre-inheritance experiences," and they prepare children for the real responsibilities they will take on later in life.

One strategy I use is to give my children "small bites." I provide them with access to small amounts of money and then mentor them on how they can manage this money.

How can you mentor, train and establish decision-making processes for successive generations?

_____

_____

_____

_____

_____

_____

_____

_____

_____

_____

_____

_____

_____

_____

_____

_____

_____

_____

_____

_____

6. Build Family Communication and Trust

Here is another great strategy from *Beating the Midas Curse* by Perry Cochell and Rod Zeeb: Build family communication and trust.

Families are more successful when everyone within the family can communicate in a safe way. Your children and grandchildren will be more likely to share their concerns with you, and their ideas for the future, if they believe you are a safe haven.

Unfortunately, in many families, older generations and younger generations—even when they grow into adulthood—do not share this sort of "adult-to-adult" conversation. Adult children believe they must defer to older generations, and a natural tension begins to build.

Therefore, create an intentional plan to open the lines of communication and trust amongst all the grown generations. Consider these questions:

- Do all family members have permission to assert themselves and take the first step to initiate communication?
- Do all family members feel safe in asserting themselves?
- Do all family members believe that what they contribute will make a difference?

If not, consider reading *Beating the Midas Curse* and *Creating the High-Performance Team* by Steve Buchholz and Thomas Roth.

7. Collaboration of Professional Advisors

To empower both your generation and subsequent generations, all the professional advisors who work on your behalf should have a shared vision of the outcomes you want for your family.

And they should meet regularly to discuss these outcomes. Otherwise, they may become the eight tentacles of an octopus that are all pulling in different directions.

Communication amongst all the professionals working on your behalf—which includes your financial advisor, your insurance advisor, your estate planning attorney, your accountant, and all other professional advisors—typically occurs via e-mail, phone, or very brief face-to-face meetings. Each professional works on his or her part of the plan, communicating with the other professionals only when asked to share information.

This is not collaborative teamwork. If you want your plan to be protected, all eight arms of the octopus must be working together toward the same vision. Your advisors cannot work in silos. They must share their expertise in their different fields so that they leverage each other's knowledge to form the best possible plans.

Sadly, effective and interdependent team collaboration of this kind is still a rare occurrence in the planning world.

One of the hallmarks of good heritage design is the selection of the advisors who will work as a fully collaborative team on your behalf. This element is critical for effectively sustaining wealth and unity from generation to generation.

8. Do It Now

Successful families take decisive action. They pro-actively address each of the elements described in this section. They do not put it off, wait for a perfect time, or move ahead only when the waters are calm and the sailing is smooth. ("Smooth waters do not make strong sailors," says the poet.)

Successful families make a commitment to their vision, and they hold fast to the commitment by putting family first. They do not put the business of the family on the backburner even when the storms of depression, recession, political chaos, or world war swirl around them. In fact, research shows that in troubled times, successful families come even closer together. In the face of crisis, they increase the pace, frequency, variety and commitment to their family activities with renewed urgency.

I've read of a family patriarch who put it this way: "There may be bad times to invest in markets, but there is never a bad time to invest in your family."

What three steps will you take this week to put your family first?

1. _____

2. _____

3. _____

Empowering the
Next Generation

Score Yourself from 1-12

Mindsets	1	2	3	4	5	6
Definition of Wealth	You define wealth as the money and assets that you have accumulated.			You have focused primarily on building financial wealth and worry that it may ruin the motivation & emotional development of your children.		
Identify Your Values	You cannot articulate your values and have no interest in discovering them.			You cannot articulate your values but feel compelled to consider them.		
Tools to Pass Along Values	You aren't a planner and have found that it's best to see what happens rather than have an outcome in mind.			You wish you had a plan to pass along your values but haven't had the time or inspiration to put it on paper.		
Family Fun and Development	You have a family full of independent thinkers who go their own direction without much interaction.			You dream of having a plan for keeping your family together through fun & growth, but don't know where to begin.		
Training & Mentoring Future Generations	You started with nothing and you want your children to benefit from the same experience.			You can see the value of exposing children to philanthropy and real world decision making but don't have a systematic plan.		
Family Communication and Trust	You are demoralized that communication is so poor in your family and don't expect it to get better now.			You worry that your family isn't communicating as well as they could and that it is negatively impacting unity and trust.		
Collaboration of Professional Advisors	You are a "do it yourselfer" and don't see much value in paying for outside advisors in estate & legacy planning.			You recognize that your planning has been done piecemeal and that your advisors rarely collaborate as a team on your behalf.		
Do It Now	You are overwhelmed by everything on your plate and have no expectation that you can address these issues in the foreseeable future.			You are irritated that you haven't addressed some or many of these issues and recognize that accountability is essential to make progress.		
Scorecard	➡	➡	➡	➡	➡	➡

7	8	9	10	11	12	Current Score	Desired Score
You have created sufficient wealth for your family and don't need to spend additional time/energy on growing it further.			You view wealth as a balance of financial, intellectual, human, and social capital. You promote balanced growth of each area.				
You are happy with whatever you know of your family history and are comfortable with where things are going in your family.			You absolutely want your values to continue in your family as a fundamental part of your legacy.				
You have a very clear vision for your family's present and future, with no plans to evolve where you're going.			You regularly re-visit your family vision and have a plan to intentionally pass it from one generation to the next.				
You are satisfied with the time your family spends together, and they don't need your help for further growth.			You are always looking for more ways to unify your family, through spontaneous fun, organized meetings, and enrichment opportunities.				
You have a written program for training and mentoring each generation. Your plan is working great.			You see training & mentoring as essential for preparing the children and regularly provide pre-inheritance experiences.				
You are proud of the levels of communication and trust in your family and can't imagine things getting better.			You value trust among family members most highly and want everyone to know that they can make positive contribution.				
You have the best advisors available and are perfectly happy with all their services.			Your professional advisors have a shared vision of the outcomes you want for your family and meet at least annually to talk just about you.				
You have done all this planning and everything is in place with no need for additional enhancements.			You know that successful families take decisive action and demand ongoing, forward action to achieve your most important goals.				

Summary
The Journey from Security and Success to Significance

The only Christmas gift that survived my childhood fire was five shares of Comdisco stock. I asked for it because my best friend's dad said it would be a great investment in my future.

After the fire took all of our belongings, including the physical presents we had unwrapped that morning, I spent many mornings checking the stock's performance in the school library's Wall Street Journal. It was a healthy distraction from the challenges of the moment.

This fortuitous beginning of my desire to create financial security for myself has had a significant impact for my family and for my clients, whom I advise in the same manner as I do myself.

Combined with my passion for meeting, befriending, and connecting great people for mutual benefit, I have the perfect career. It allows me to learn everyone's story, understand their hopes and dreams for the future, and leverage my network of internal experts at Northwestern Mutual, as well as external experts in every field to help my clients lead their life by design, sooner than anyone expects.

My hope is that we can partner with you in creating financial security, success and significance. I invite you to continue this journey by completing our attached scorecards for measuring where you are in each of the previous eight strategies in each life domain. You can also complete them online at www.smartmoney.vip, where I will receive a copy of your results so that I can share what I have learned so that you can begin to protect your family as quickly as possible.

This is certainly just the beginning of our process for helping move families to success and beyond—to significance. I would be happy to share our entire process and all of our tools with you.

Please contact me at: curtis.estes@nm.com or call directly at (310) 903-5088.

References and Interesting Reads

- *Beating the Midas Curse*
  by Perry L. Cochell & Rod Zeeb

- *Grit*
  by Angela Duckworth

- *Family First*
  by Curtis Estes

- *Your Life by Design*
  by Curtis Estes

- *Family Wealth*
  by Jay Hughes

- *Rhythm of Life*
  by Matthew Kelly

- *Unique Ability*
  by Catherine Nomura

- *Creating the High-Performance Team*
  by Steve Buchholz and Thomas Roth

Acknowledgments

I would like to thank, first and foremost, Kristi Estes, for always supporting me in everything I do, and Jordan, Vyvien and Christian, who bring me immense joy every day.

I extend infinite gratitude, as well, to David Adams, who has shared his years of wisdom as the steward of an incredible family legacy, and Juan Baron, my faithful early morning workout partner.

Thanks to Jocelyn Baker for keeping us on track and moving this project forward, and to Steve Braun, for reading every word and providing valued perspective.

"Appreciate" isn't a strong enough word for Ethan Frey and Tony Stacy, who have provided daily inspiration. Thank you also to Brady Beaubien, Tyler Barth, Patrick Sells, and Jeff Benton, with whom my bigger future is just beginning.

Amir Mossanen, you are a true thought-leader in serving great families.

And finally, thank you to my Titan Society partners and our 25-year journey together, becoming the best version of ourselves.

About the Author
Curtis Estes

Curtis Estes is Kristi's husband and Jordan, Vyvien, and Christian's dad. He is actively involved with the National Center for Fathering, a member of the Bel Air Presbyterian Church, and a supporter of Saving Innocence and the Internal Justice Mission. He's been trustee for Spokane's Whitworth University and is currently on the board at Pacifica Christian High School.

A CFP® Certificant, he began his professional career in 1991 with Northwestern Mutual. He graduated from the University of Kansas with a degree in journalism. Curtis is the author of *Your Life by Design: A Step-by-Step Guide to Creating a Bigger Future* and *Family First: How to Be a Hero at Home.*

He's a grateful steward of the gold key to the Secret Table.

We'd love to support you in your efforts to enjoy more financial security, success and significance.
curtis.estes@nm.com • 310-903-5088

Made in the USA
Middletown, DE
18 September 2023

38222272R00058